Questions and Answers About
DINOSAURS

DOUGAL DIXON

Kingfisher

NEW YORK

KINGFISHER
Larousse Kingfisher Chambers Inc.
95 Madison Avenue
New York, New York 10016

First American edition 1995
10 9 8 7 6 5 4 3 2 1 (HC)
10 9 8 7 6 5 4 3 2 (PB)

Library of Congress Cataloging-in-Publication Data
Dixon, Dougal.
Questions and answers about dinosaurs / by Dougal Dixon. –
1st American ed.
p. cm. – (Questions and answers about)
Includes index.
1. Dinosaurs – Miscellanea – Juvenile literature.   [1. Dinosaurs –
Miscellanea.   2. Questions and answers.]   I. Title   II. Series.
QE862.D5D554   1995
567.9'1–dc20   CIP AC

Editor: Jackie Gaff
Series designer: Terry Woodley
Designer: David West Children's Book Designers
Illustrators: Robby Braun (p. 20); Chris Forsey (pp. 4–5,
21, insets pp. 6–7, 16–19, 28 bottom, 31 top); Steve Kirk
(pp. 10–11, 18–19, 22–5, 28–9); Bernard Long, Temple Rogers
(pp. 2–3, 16–17, 30–3, 36–8); Doreen McGuinness, Garden
Studio (pp. 6–7, 12); Myke Taylor, Garden Studio (pp. 8–9,
13, 14–15, 26–7, 34–5).
Cover illustration: Andrew Robinson

ISBN 1-85697-554-1 (HC)
ISBN 1-85697-553-3 (PB)

Printed and bound in Spain

CONTENTS

How do we know about ancient life?

Clues about ancient life are hidden in the Earth's crust. Most rocks are made up of layers of mud and sand, rather like a giant sandwich. Over millions of years, the layers were squeezed and cemented together, eventually becoming hard. The bones and shells of animals trapped in the layers also turned to stone, forming fossils. Scientists learn about ancient life by studying fossils and the rocks in which they are found.

2 The position of each bone is recorded, to help scientists piece the animal back together later on.

1 The fossilized bones of ancient animals can easily be damaged. Great care is taken when uncovering them.

3 Photographs are also taken, both of the way the fossilized skeleton is lying, and of the rock and soil layers.

DISCOVERY FACTS

● In 1810, 12-year-old Mary Anning and her brother Joseph became the first people to find the fossilized skeleton of a sea reptile, later named an ichthyosaur (see page 31).

4 Each fossilized bone is encased in a layer of plaster of Paris. This protects it on its way to the museum.

HOW FOSSILS FORM

1 The dead body of an animal sinks to the bottom of a lake, river, or sea.

2 Its skeleton is buried by layers of sand and mud. Millions of years now pass.

3 The sand and mud turn to rock. The bones become fossils.

4 In time, the rocks wear away and the fossil appears at the surface.

When did life begin?

The Earth is so old that most of its history is a mystery to us. However, scientists believe that the Earth began about 4.6 billion years ago, and that life first appeared about a billion years later.

The oldest fossils ever found date back to 600 million years ago. It wasn't until then that animals developed the hard shells and bones that could form fossils. The soft bodies of earlier animals just rotted away.

With their long stalks, crinoids looked like plants. They were really animals, the relatives of today's starfish.

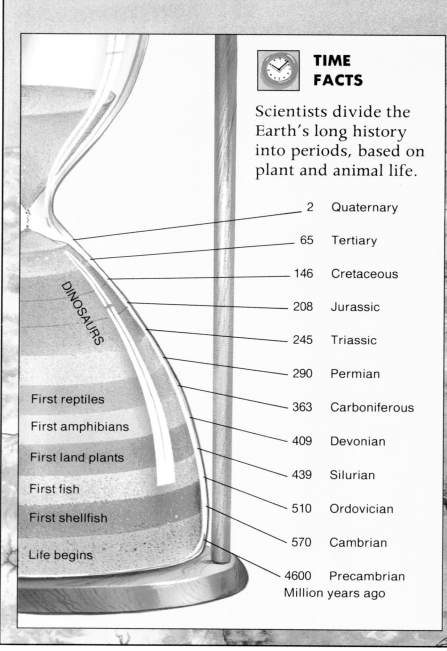

TIME FACTS

Scientists divide the Earth's long history into periods, based on plant and animal life.

2	Quaternary
65	Tertiary
146	Cretaceous
208	Jurassic
245	Triassic
290	Permian
363	Carboniferous
409	Devonian
439	Silurian
510	Ordovician
570	Cambrian
4600	Precambrian

Million years ago

DINOSAURS

First reptiles

First amphibians

First land plants

First fish

First shellfish

Life begins

Calcichordates were related to crinoids. They crawled along the seabed, pushing with their tails.

Some of the oldest fossils ever found are of the coiled shells of sea snails rather like the whelks of today.

The Silurian seas must have been full of the animals we call graptolites. Their fossils are quite common.

All Silurian animals lived in the sea. Trilobites prowled for food on the seabed. They were rather like early crabs.

Early corals looked like sea anemones in shells. They were the ancestors of today's corals.

 EVOLVE AN ANIMAL

There are two main groups of animal today —those with back-bones and those without. Backboned animals didn't develop until Silurian times. Here's how to trace what happened:

1 Make a tadpole-like creature out of modeling clay.

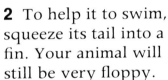

2 To help it to swim, squeeze its tail into a fin. Your animal will still be very floppy.

3 Stiffen it by pushing in a pencil backbone.

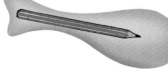

Living things develop and change very, very slowly, over millions of years. We call this long, slow process of change "evolution."

What were the first fish like?

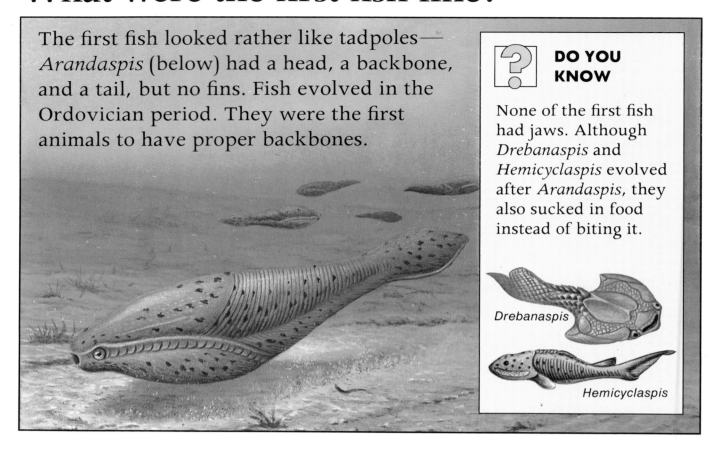

The first fish looked rather like tadpoles—*Arandaspis* (below) had a head, a backbone, and a tail, but no fins. Fish evolved in the Ordovician period. They were the first animals to have proper backbones.

Which fish was as big as a whale?

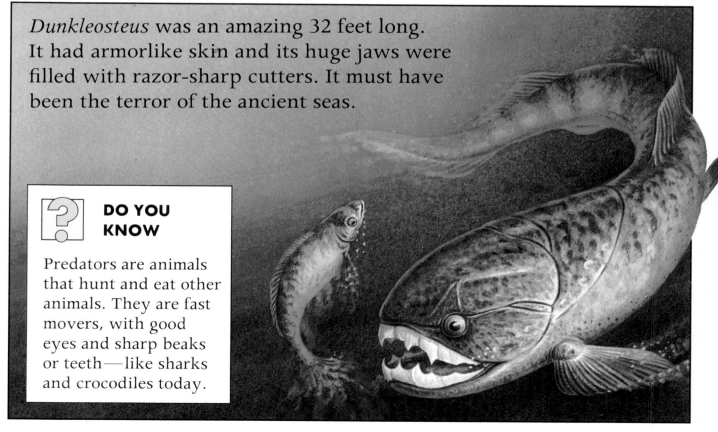

Dunkleosteus was an amazing 32 feet long. It had armorlike skin and its huge jaws were filled with razor-sharp cutters. It must have been the terror of the ancient seas.

How old are sharks?

Sharks form one of the oldest animal groups alive today. Their ancestors developed 400 million years ago, in the Devonian seas.

Stethacanthus (below) was a very odd-looking shark that lived about 300 million years ago.

Cladoselache was one of the first sharks, evolving even before *Stethacanthus*.

Xenacanthus also appeared in Devonian times, but it outlived the other two types.

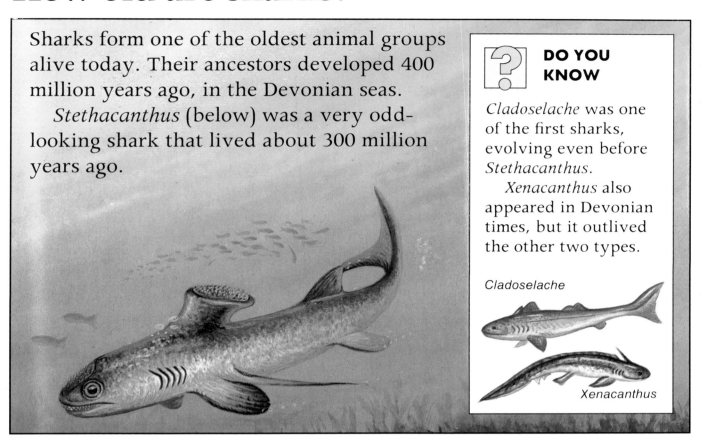

Cladoselache

Xenacanthus

Which fish could breathe out of water?

At the same time as sharks were evolving, other fish, called lungfish, were developing a way of breathing air and living on dry land. They were probably tempted ashore by the insects that were now living there.

Panderichthys was an early land-going lungfish. To help them move on land, these fish developed sturdy fleshy fins.

As well as gills for breathing in water, lungfish had lungs for breathing in air.

Which were the first landlubbers?

Lungfish were only able to live on land for short periods of time. Gradually, however, new animals evolved which could spend most of their lives out of water—the amphibians. Amphibians could breathe air and, as they spent more and more time on land, their fleshy fins slowly evolved into strong legs. They couldn't live far from water, though, or their slimy skins dried out. They laid their eggs in water, too.

DO YOU KNOW

Ichthyostega was an early amphibian. Like its fish ancestors, it had a fish's head and a tail with a fin. But it had legs instead of fleshy fins, and feet with toes, showing that it lived mostly on land.

Eryops was the size of a pig. Its thick skin was like armor, and helped to support its body weight on land.

Eogyrinus must have spent a lot of its life in water—its tail was finlike, and its legs were short.

Eogyrinus was as long as a car. It lived like a crocodile, chasing fish through the swamp waters.

- The word amphibian means "leading a double life."

- Amphibians spend only part of their lives on land. They must lay their eggs in water and spend the early part of their lives as swimming animals.

- Newts and toads are modern amphibians.

All sorts of different amphibians evolved during the Carboniferous period. The land was covered with forests of treelike ferns at that time.

Keraterpeton was a small salamanderlike amphibian with a long tail. It probably ate insects.

Phlegethonia had no legs. It burrowed like a worm through the rotting vegetation of the forest floor.

11

When were dragonflies as big as birds?

Huge flying insects lived at the same time as the amphibians in the thick Carboniferous forests. Dragonflies the size of birds flew around the forest swamps, and many different kinds of crawling insects thrived in the lush vegetation. Insects were among the first animals to live on dry land, attracted by the new plants growing there.

The damp Carboniferous forests must have been buzzing with the sound of flying insects. The lush plant life provided them with plenty of food.

CRAWLER FACTS

● *Brontoscorpio* (below) was as big as a cat. Like many of the first scorpions, it could live both on land and in the water.

● The giant millipede *Arthropleura* (above) was nearly 6 feet long. It fed on rotting vegetation in the ferny undergrowth.

Meganeura was probably the biggest dragonfly ever. It had a wingspan of 27 inches —that's the same as a modern parrot's!

When did the first reptiles appear?

Reptiles began to evolve about 350 million years ago. They were different from the amphibians in a very important way. Although amphibians are suited to life on land, they always have to return to the water to lay their eggs—these have to stay moist. Reptiles' eggs can be laid on land because they are protected by a leathery shell. Reptiles were the first true land-dwellers.

REPTILE FACTS

● The first reptile was *Westlothiana*, a lizard-like animal about 4 inches long. It lived among the amphibians in the Carboniferous forests.

Westlothiana

Coelurosauravus was a gliding reptile about the size of a frisbee.

The slow-moving reptile *Pareiasaurus* was as big as a cow. Its broad mouth was just right for chewing tough plants.

Where did mammals come from?

Mammals evolved from a group of animals called mammal-like reptiles. These reptiles had differently shaped teeth for killing and chewing. Over millions of years, their legs became straighter, holding the animal clear of the ground. By the end of the Triassic period, they had developed into the mammals themselves.

Megazostrodon was one of the first mammals. Like many modern mammals, it had warm fur, and whiskers to help it feel its way about.

Mammals do not lay eggs, but give birth to young animals. The babies feed on their mother's milk.

FAMILY FACTS

Dimetrodon

● *Lycaenops* was the size of a small dog. *Massetognathus* was one of the last of the mammal-like reptiles, and among the first to have fur on its body.

● *Dimetrodon* was one of the first mammal-like reptiles. The stiff fin on its back gave off heat and kept the animal cool.

Lycaenops

Massetognathus

What were ruling reptiles?

The animal group that we call the ruling reptiles lived at the same time as the mammal-like reptiles. They had strong hind legs and long tails, and looked rather like crocodiles. The animals that evolved from them belonged to three different groups. One group evolved into the crocodiles, another into the pterosaurs (see page 28), and a third into the dinosaurs.

(see page 28)

DO YOU KNOW

Today's crocodiles still have the sharp teeth, long tail and strong legs of their distant ancestors, such as *Chasmatosaurus*, one of the first ruling reptiles.

Chasmatosaurus

Crocodile

Ornithosuchus was one of the later ruling reptiles. It lived on land, and could walk upright on two legs, using its long tail for balance.

Ornithosuchus may have gone on two legs only when it ran, spending the rest of the time on all fours.

When did dinosaurs first appear?

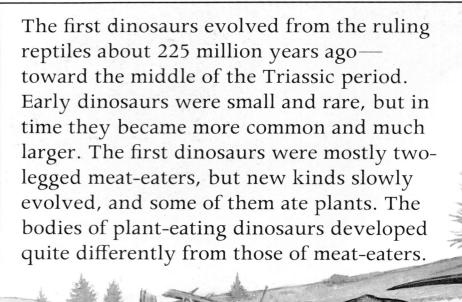

The first dinosaurs evolved from the ruling reptiles about 225 million years ago—toward the middle of the Triassic period. Early dinosaurs were small and rare, but in time they became more common and much larger. The first dinosaurs were mostly two-legged meat-eaters, but new kinds slowly evolved, and some of them ate plants. The bodies of plant-eating dinosaurs developed quite differently from those of meat-eaters.

Insects and lizards were a tasty meal in the deserts where *Procompsognathus* lived. But it had to catch them first!

Procompsognathus was one of the first dinosaurs. About the size of a vulture, it chased its prey on its long hind legs.

 EATING FACTS

● Early dinosaurs were two-legged meat-eaters like *Procompsognathus*. Four-legged plant-eaters like *Plateosaurus* evolved later. Plants are tougher to digest than meat—it takes longer to break them down and get the goodness out.

The conifers eaten by some dinosaurs were very hard to digest.

● In animals, digestion takes place in a long tube off the stomach, called the intestine. Plant-eating dinosaurs evolved longer intestines, and huge bodies to fit them in! Their size meant they had to go on four legs instead of two. Two-legged plant-eaters evolved much later.

Plateosaurus was one of the first of the large plant-eating dinosaurs. Its long neck helped it to nibble the treetops.

Plateosaurus walked on all fours, but could stand on its hind legs to feed. It was about 25 feet long.

 HIP FACTS

- Scientists divide dinosaurs by the shape of their hip bones. There are two main groups—lizard-hipped and bird-hipped. All the meat-eaters and the really big four-legged plant-eaters were lizard-hipped.

Albertosaurus (lizard-hipped meat-eater)

Alamosaurus (lizard-hipped plant-eater)

- The bird-hipped dinosaurs evolved later. They were all plant-eaters—both two-legged and four-legged ones.

Kritosaurus (bird-hipped)

Which were the giant dinosaurs?

The long-necked plant-eaters that evolved from *Plateosaurus* were the largest land animals of all time. Some were more than ten times the size of an elephant. Known as sauropods, these giants thrived at the end of the Jurassic period, when the lush plant life provided plenty of good food.

Sauropods had big bodies with a long neck and a tiny head. They could reach the treetops to feed on their diet of leaves and twigs. At their size, they must have spent nearly all their time just eating!

Brachiosaurus was one of the tallest dinosaurs. It could raise its head 42 feet above ground — that's as high as a four-story building!

SIZE FACTS

● *Mamenchisaurus* had the longest neck ever. At 50 feet, it was longer than four cars parked end to end.

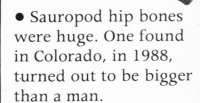

● Sauropod hip bones were huge. One found in Colorado, in 1988, turned out to be bigger than a man.

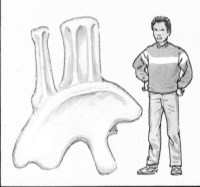

Apatosaurus was 70 feet long. Its tail made up nearly half its body length, and may have been lashed like a whip to frighten off attackers.

DINOSAUR PRINTS

How to make perfect prehistoric prints!

1 Cut a potato in two and draw a dinosaur shape on each surface —practice this first.

2 Very carefully, cut round your shape with a knife, so that it is slightly raised.

3 Coat your dinosaur with paint, and print!

A long neck and tail made *Diplodocus* one of the longest dinosaurs. At 90 feet, it was equal to seven cars parked end to end!

Were all dinosaurs huge?

We usually think of dinosaurs as huge monsters, the size of houses. In fact, many were quite small. Some were no bigger than today's lizards and songbirds.

These dinosaurs included plant-eaters, and meat-eaters that fed on insects or on animals even smaller than themselves.

DO YOU KNOW

Dinosaur names are Latin. They are often long, and hard to say. Many of them simply describe a dinosaur's appearance. For example, *Styracosaurus* means "spiked reptile."

Compsognathus had a thin tail which was more than twice as long as its body.

Compsognathus was about the size of a chicken, and fast on its feet. It was a meat-eater and fed on small lizards.

DO YOU KNOW

Scutellosaurus was another tiny dinosaur—it would only have been the size of a cat if it were alive today! Rows of studs protected this plant-eater along its back and tail.

Where was the smallest skeleton found?

A skeleton small enough to fit in your hand was found in Argentina, South America, in 1979. Scientists thought they had discovered the smallest dinosaur ever, but it turned out to be the skeleton of a baby dinosaur.

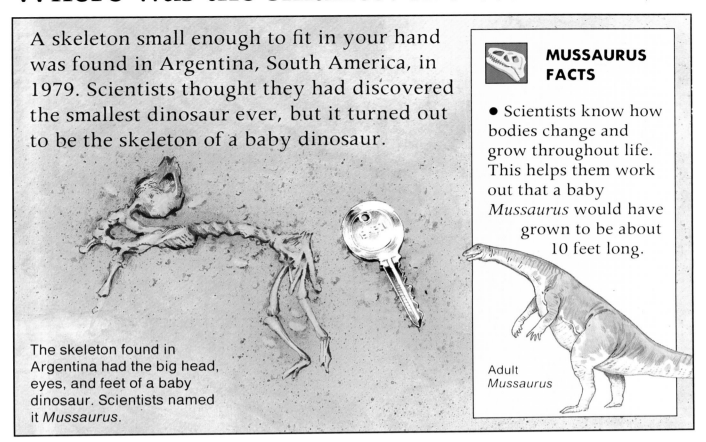

The skeleton found in Argentina had the big head, eyes, and feet of a baby dinosaur. Scientists named it *Mussaurus*.

MUSSAURUS FACTS

● Scientists know how bodies change and grow throughout life. This helps them work out that a baby *Mussaurus* would have grown to be about 10 feet long.

Adult *Mussaurus*

Where was the smallest footprint found?

A dinosaur footprint no bigger than a modern sparrow's was discovered among rocks in Nova Scotia, Canada, in the 1980s. Reptiles don't live there today, as it's much too cold. The climate must have been warmer 150 million years ago!

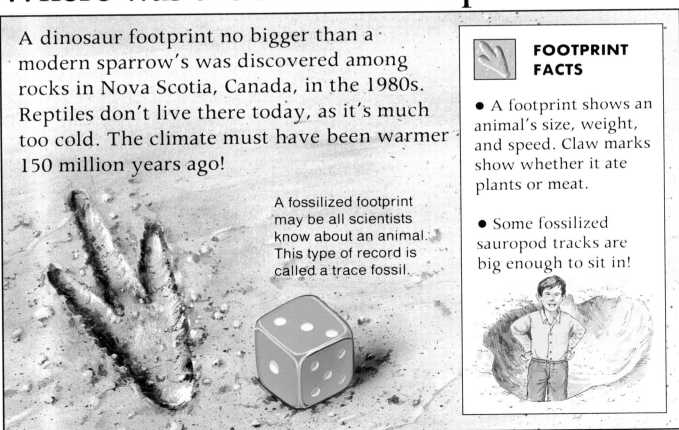

A fossilized footprint may be all scientists know about an animal. This type of record is called a trace fossil.

FOOTPRINT FACTS

● A footprint shows an animal's size, weight, and speed. Claw marks show whether it ate plants or meat.

● Some fossilized sauropod tracks are big enough to sit in!

Which were the fastest dinosaurs?

The meat-eaters were the fastest of all the dinosaurs because of the way their bodies were built. They moved on strong hind legs, balanced by a heavy tail. This allowed them to run very quickly, which helped them to catch their supper! Hunters always have to run faster than their prey—otherwise they simply won't eat enough to survive.

Troodon held its long tail out stiffly as it ran, making a perfect balance for its long neck, and helping it run at top speed.

The fierce meat-eating dinosaur *Troodon* was the size of an emu. It could run at speed on its long hind legs.

SPEED FACTS

● *Struthiomimus* was one of the fastest dinosaurs. It was about the size and shape of an ostrich, and with its huge stride, it may have run as fast as 30 miles per hour.

Ostrich

Troodon was a deadly hunter. The huge curved claw on each hind foot was used to slash its prey to death.

Struthio-mimus

Which were the deadliest dinosaurs?

The meat-eating dinosaurs weren't just fast—they were the most ferocious animals that have ever lived. As time went on, larger and faster kinds evolved. *Tyrannosaurus* was the biggest of them all, measuring over 40 feet —about the length of three cars! With its powerful legs and razorlike jaws, it must have been a terrifyingly efficient killer.

Tyrannosaurus's head was more than 3 feet long. Its deadly teeth were as big and as jagged as steak knives.

Tyrannosaurus's arms were surprisingly small. Each hand had only two clawed fingers, possibly used for picking its teeth.

Tyrannosaurus had strong legs with huge feet. They had to be sturdy enough to carry the dinosaur's great bulk while it attacked.

MEAT-EATER FACTS

● *Spinosaurus* lived in Africa. It was as long as *Tyrannosaurus*, but more lightly built.

Why did some dinosaurs have horns?

Plant-eating dinosaurs needed to protect themselves from fierce meat-eaters like *Tyrannosaurus*. Some kinds developed horns to scare off their attackers. *Triceratops* (below) had three vicious-looking horns.

HORN FACTS

- Horned dinosaurs are called ceratopsians. *Styracosaurus* had a sharp spiky collar. *Pachyrhinosaurus* had a bony knob on its nose.

Styracosaurus

Pachyrhinosaurus

Which dinosaurs had armor?

Instead of horns, some plant-eaters had thick skin which protected them like armor. These dinosaurs were called ankylosaurs. Bony spikes grew in their skin. Some even had a bony club on the end of their tail.

With one charge of its shoulder spikes, *Panoplosaurus* could seriously injure a hungry meat-eater.

What was a bonehead?

Boneheads were a group of dinosaurs with very thick skulls. They used to head-butt one another to decide who would lead the herd, like mountain goats do today. The thick skull protected the soft brain inside.

With its thick skull and stiff backbone, a bonehead was like a living battering ram.

Which dinosaurs had back plates?

Stegosaurus (below) was the largest of the stegosaurs, a group of plant-eating dinosaurs with plates and spines down their backs.

STEGOSAUR FACTS

● The stegosaurs' plates and spines may have been used as armor, or for giving off heat from the animal's body.

Wuerhosaurus

Kentrosaurus

Did dinosaurs lay eggs?

Like most reptiles today, young dinosaurs hatched out of eggs. Scientists have found groups of fossilized nests, some containing ten eggs or more. The eggs are small for such large animals. Smaller eggs have thinner shells, making it easier for the animal to hatch out.

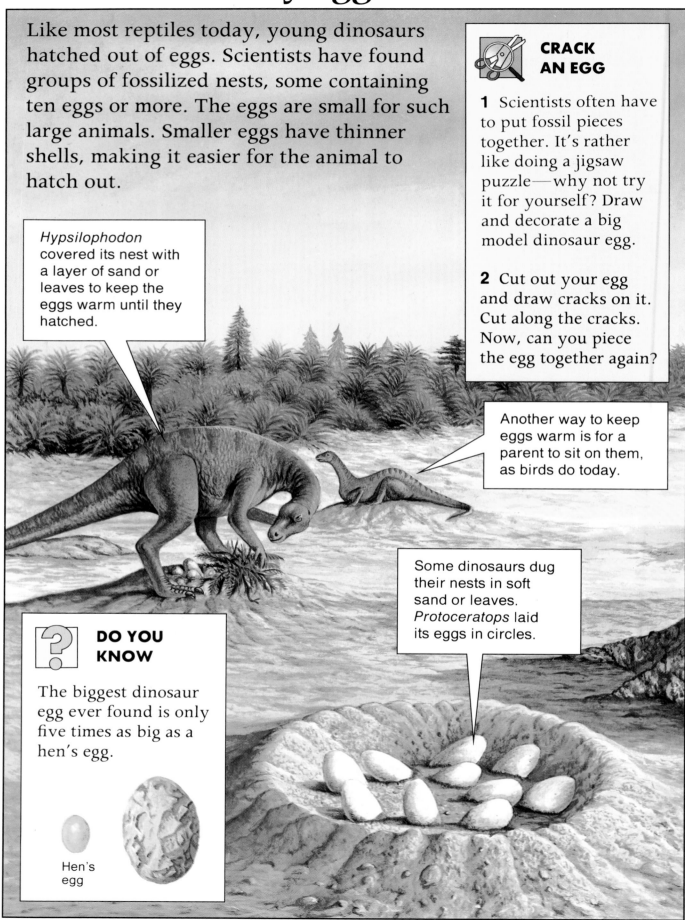

CRACK AN EGG

1 Scientists often have to put fossil pieces together. It's rather like doing a jigsaw puzzle—why not try it for yourself? Draw and decorate a big model dinosaur egg.

2 Cut out your egg and draw cracks on it. Cut along the cracks. Now, can you piece the egg together again?

Hypsilophodon covered its nest with a layer of sand or leaves to keep the eggs warm until they hatched.

Another way to keep eggs warm is for a parent to sit on them, as birds do today.

Some dinosaurs dug their nests in soft sand or leaves. *Protoceratops* laid its eggs in circles.

DO YOU KNOW

The biggest dinosaur egg ever found is only five times as big as a hen's egg.

Hen's egg

26

What were baby dinosaurs like?

Newborn dinosaurs were as helpless as baby birds. They were fed by their parents until they were big enough to leave the nest.

Fossilized nests containing baby dinosaurs were found in the United States in 1978. By studying them, scientists learned a lot about the young of the dinosaur called *Maiasaura*.

MAIASAURA FACTS

● *Maiasaura* means "good mother lizard."

● They lived in herds, looking after their young together, and nesting at the same site each year.

The babies were fed by their parents until they could look after themselves.

Baby dinosaurs may have had a small horn on their nose to help them break out of the eggshell.

Tiny baby *Maiasaura*, as well as unhatched eggs, have been found in some of the fossilized nests.

Could dinosaurs fly?

Dinosaurs were land animals—they couldn't fly. Another group of animals ruled the skies in dinosaur times. Called pterosaurs, they had large heads, small furry bodies, and leathery wings. They didn't have feathers. There were many kinds of pterosaur. The ones shown here all lived in Europe about 150 million years ago.

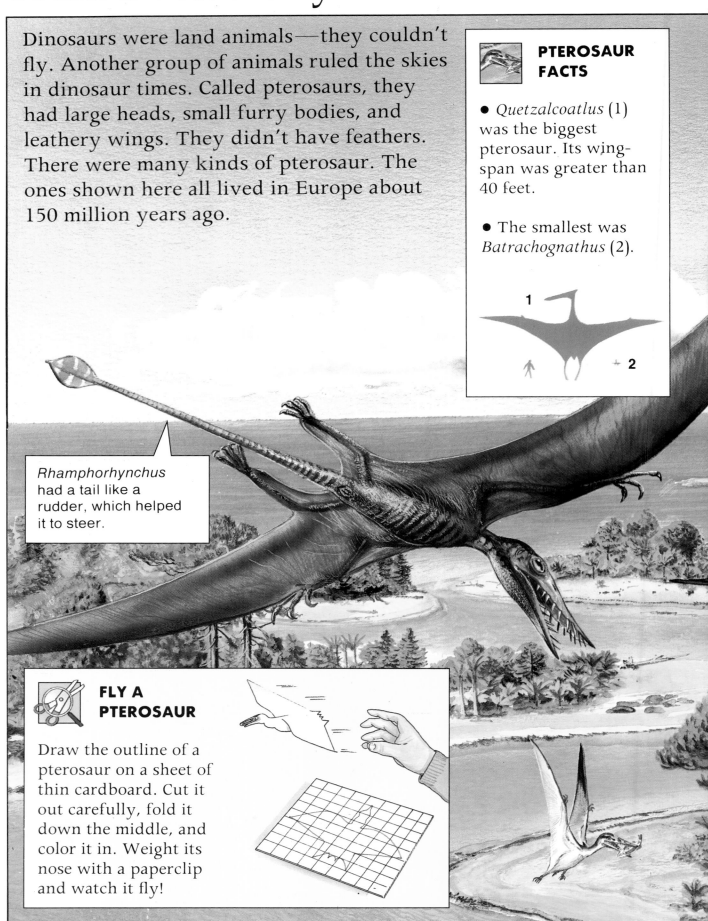

PTEROSAUR FACTS

● *Quetzalcoatlus* (1) was the biggest pterosaur. Its wingspan was greater than 40 feet.

● The smallest was *Batrachognathus* (2).

1

2

Rhamphorhynchus had a tail like a rudder, which helped it to steer.

FLY A PTEROSAUR

Draw the outline of a pterosaur on a sheet of thin cardboard. Cut it out carefully, fold it down the middle, and color it in. Weight its nose with a paperclip and watch it fly!

Archaeopteryx was the first bird. It was covered with feathers, but it had teeth, not a beak.

Anurognathus was one of the smallest pterosaurs. It had a short snout and tiny teeth. It ate insects.

DO YOU KNOW

Scientists can tell what a pterosaur ate by studying its jaws.

Dzungaripterus had a beak like pincers for crushing shellfish.

Dimorphodon had the strong jaws and sharp teeth of a meat-eater.

Tropeognathus fed on fish. Its curious jaws steadied it in the water.

Pterodactylus had broad wings. Like many pterosaurs, it fed on fish.

Could dinosaurs swim?

Dinosaurs couldn't swim, but there were many seagoing reptiles during the dinosaur age. The biggest belonged to a group of short- or long-necked animals with four flippers—the plesiosaurs.

Fossils of sea creatures are fairly common because their bodies naturally sank to the seabed and were buried in mud, which later turned to stone. A land animal's body had to fall into a river or lake first (see page 5).

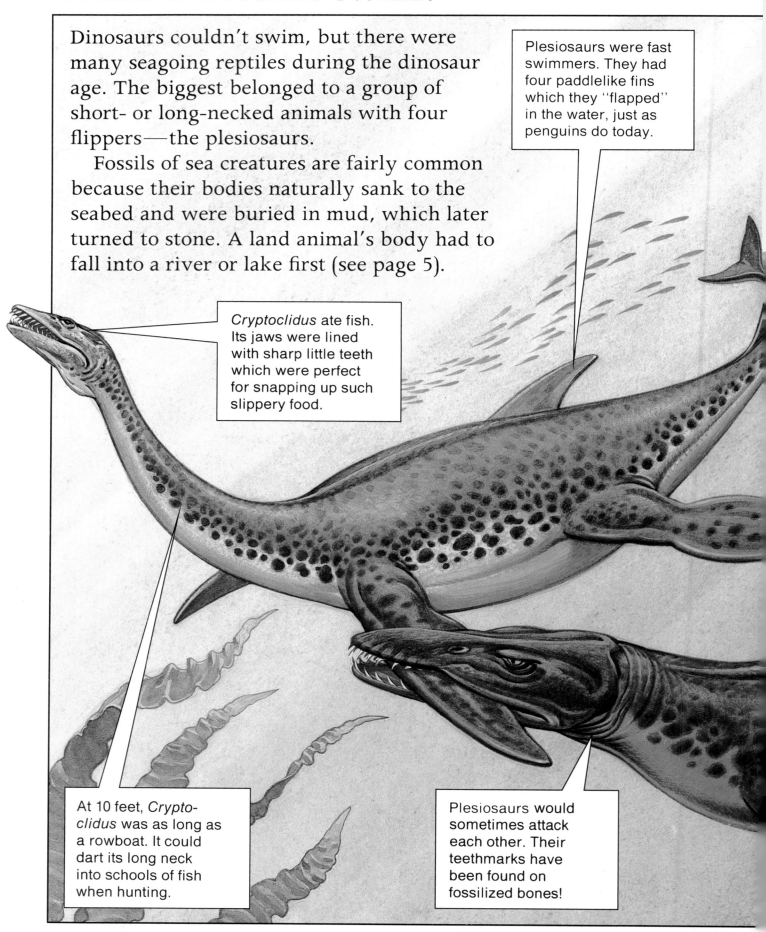

Plesiosaurs were fast swimmers. They had four paddlelike fins which they "flapped" in the water, just as penguins do today.

Cryptoclidus ate fish. Its jaws were lined with sharp little teeth which were perfect for snapping up such slippery food.

At 10 feet, *Cryptoclidus* was as long as a rowboat. It could dart its long neck into schools of fish when hunting.

Plesiosaurs would sometimes attack each other. Their teethmarks have been found on fossilized bones!

TEST OUT BODY SHAPE

Animals' bodies evolve to suit their surround-ings. Sea animals' rounded bodies move through water easily.

1 Collect together some differently shaped objects.

2 Tie string to each one and tow it through water. Which object moves most easily?

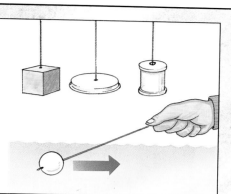

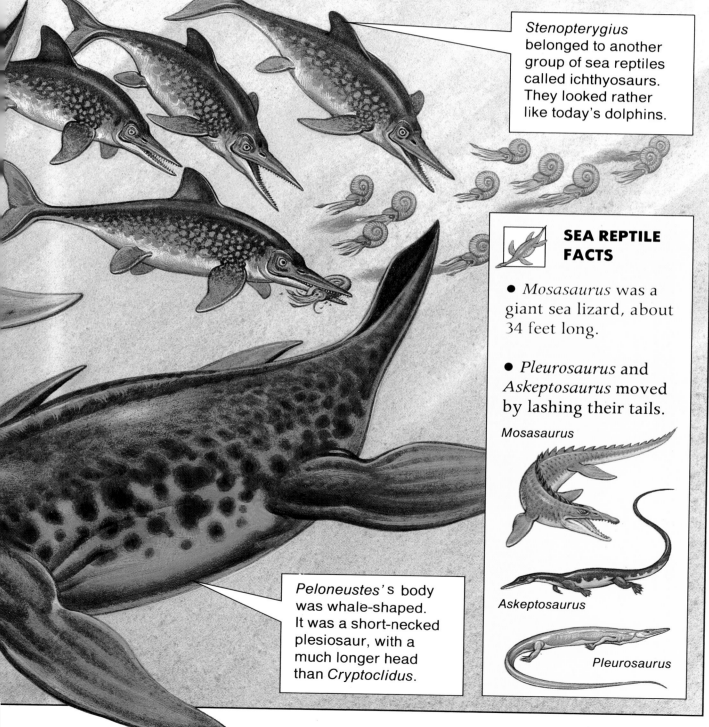

Stenopterygius belonged to another group of sea reptiles called ichthyosaurs. They looked rather like today's dolphins.

SEA REPTILE FACTS

● *Mosasaurus* was a giant sea lizard, about 34 feet long.

● *Pleurosaurus* and *Askeptosaurus* moved by lashing their tails.

Mosasaurus

Askeptosaurus

Pleurosaurus

Peloneustes's body was whale-shaped. It was a short-necked plesiosaur, with a much longer head than *Cryptoclidus*.

What happened to the dinosaurs?

Suddenly they all disappeared. Dinosaurs seem to have vanished after the Cretaceous period—along with pterosaurs, sea reptiles, and many other animals. No fossils of them have ever been found in any rock younger than 65 million years old.

Scientists aren't sure what happened. Some think that giant rocks from outer space crashed into Earth sending up huge clouds of dust. Others have different ideas.

The huge dust clouds sent up by the crashing rocks would have blocked out the Sun, plunging the world into freezing darkness, and killing many of the animals very quickly.

Birds managed to survive the disaster. Maybe they were able to hide from the choking dust until it cleared.

EXTINCTION FACTS

● Some scientists think changes in the Sun's rays weakened dinosaur eggshells and killed their young.

● Earth's continents were once closer than they are today. Dinosaurs moved from one to another and may have spread disease.

● Dinosaurs may have been poisoned by new kinds of trees and flowering plants.

Mammals survived as well. Panic-stricken, they may have burrowed underground—perhaps hibernating until life returned to normal.

What came after the dinosaurs?

The dinosaurs had been the ruling animals on Earth for 160 million years. When they died out, the mammals began to take over. Mammals were small, but evolved quickly. *Hyaenodon* (below) was a fierce meat-eater.

? DO YOU KNOW

Meat-eating mammals such as wolves kill their prey with long teeth near the front of their mouths. Their back teeth shear the meat—they work rather like scissors.

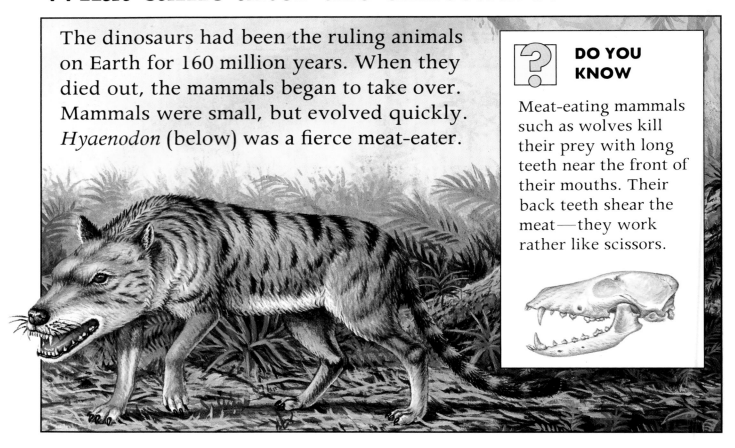

Which were the biggest mammals?

A group of plant-eating mammals known as uintatheres were the giants of their day. *Uintatherium* (below) was up to 13 feet long. The group evolved 10 million years after the dinosaurs, but later died out.

? DO YOU KNOW

Unlike meat-eaters, plant-eaters don't have long killing teeth. They have teeth that chop and grind their food, breaking it down before they swallow it.

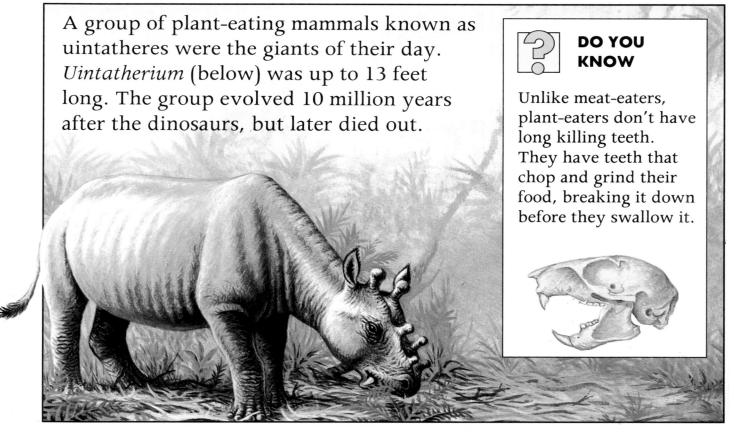

What were the first whales like?

With its small head and serpentlike body, *Basilosaurus* (below) looked very different from the whales of today. This huge sea mammal had fierce-looking teeth, and hunted fish and squid.

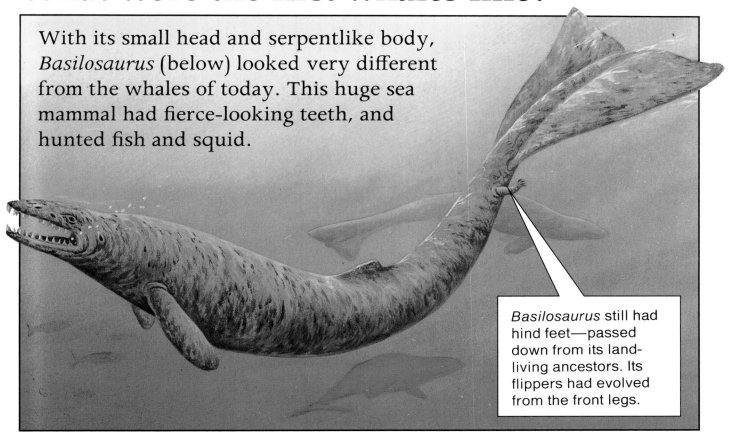

Basilosaurus still had hind feet—passed down from its land-living ancestors. Its flippers had evolved from the front legs.

What were the first bats like?

In many ways *Icaronycteris* (below) was like modern bats—its wings were made of skin, and its sharp teeth snapped up insects as it flew. It had a long tail, however—quite different from bats today.

Unlike bats today, *Icaronycteris* had a claw on its first finger as well as its thumb. It hung from these when it roosted.

When did grassland mammals appear?

About 25 million years ago, Earth's climate became cooler and drier, changing the landscape from forest to open grasslands. Some mammals changed as well, evolving in new ways to suit life on the grasslands.

Horses, for example, had been small forest animals, feeding on soft leaves and hiding from the meat-eaters. Now, they evolved to the size of sheep, with longer legs to run from their enemies on the open plains.

Grassy plains grow in dry climates. Their underground root or stem systems are able to survive drought and fire, sprouting new growth when the damage is over.

Daenodon was a distant relative of the pig. This giant animal left the forest to live on the grasslands.

DO YOU KNOW

The bodies of most grass-eating animals are fairly similar. They all need certain things to help them survive on the plains.

Many grass-eaters have long necks.

Heavy jaws are good for chewing tough grass. An elongated head keeps an animal's eyes above grass level as it feeds, and a long neck lets it see danger coming. Its long legs allow it to make a quick escape.

Parahippus was a sheep-sized horse. Its big teeth allowed it to chew the new tough grasses.

Moropus fed on leaves. To our eyes, it was very strange-looking—a cross between a horse, camel, and bear.

Trees grew here and there on the plains, and taller animals evolved to feed on their leaves, just as giraffes do today.

Syndyoceras had long legs and light hooves. Its speed and its impressive horns helped it to survive on the plains.

The fast-moving Stenomylus was an early camel, living in herds on the plains.

What was the Ice Age?

About 2 million years ago, Earth's climate became very cold. Snow and ice spread down from the North Pole over Europe and North America. This was the Ice Age. Many animals died out in the big freeze, but others managed to survive. These animals were large, with woolly coats and a thick layer of body fat to keep out the cold.

Woolly mammoths were close relatives of the elephant. They had hairy coats and long curved tusks.

Coelodonta was a huge woolly rhino-ceros. Its shaggy coat helped it to survive the icy cold.

The great Irish deer, *Megaloceros* had giant antlers nearly 13 feet across. It fed on grass and other plants.

In the Ice Age a new animal appeared. It was a mammal, and it could make tools, and hunt. This was our ancestor.

ICE AGE FACTS

● Much of the sea froze into ice and floated on the surface, making the sea level 300 feet lower than it is today—a difference of 10 two-story houses!

● There have been several ice ages in the past 2 million years. Each one was followed by warmer weather.

Useful words

Amphibians One of the main groups of animals with backbones. Amphibians live in water and on land. They include frogs, toads, and newts.

Ankylosaurs A group of dinosaurs which had a body armor of bony spines and knobs growing in their skin. *Panoplosaurus* was an ankylosaur.

Ceratopsians A group of armored dinosaurs with horns on their heads. *Triceratops* belonged to this group.

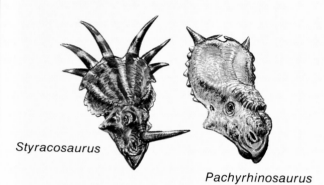

Styracosaurus

Pachyrhinosaurus

Evolution The process whereby plants and animals change and develop slowly over millions of years.

Extinction When a kind of plant or animal dies and vanishes from the Earth forever, as the dinosaur did 65 million years ago.

Fossil Plant and animal remains from millions of years ago, which have turned to stone. Scientists have learned about ancient life by studying fossils.

Ichthyosaurs A group of dolphinlike reptiles that lived in the seas during the age of the dinosaurs.

Invertebrates Animals that do not have a backbone. Jellyfish, worms, and insects are all invertebrates.

Mammals A group of animals that give birth to their young and feed them on milk from the mother's body. Human beings are mammals, as are cats, rabbits, horses, and whales.

Parahippus

Prehistoric Belonging to ancient times, thousands and millions of years before human history.

Pterosaurs A group of flying reptiles which lived in the dinosaur age. They were not birds, and their wings were covered in skin, not feathers.

Reptiles One of the main groups of animals with a backbone. Reptiles have dry scaly skin and, unlike amphibians, they lay their eggs on land. Crocodiles, snakes, and turtles are all reptiles.

Stegosaurs A group of dinosaurs that had a body armor of bony plates on their backs. *Stegosaurus* (below) belonged to this group.

Stegosaurus

Index